AF448631

Need Some Fashion Assistance?

By Kathryn Hoover

Copyright © 2023 Kathryn Hoover
All rights reserved.

Contents

My Background

I was once told by someone, who knew that I love to design, especially interior designing, that I would be good for helping other people find their fashion styles; especially those who come from very religious and legalistic backgrounds who are now trying to figure out who they are and what they like and how to make sense of the world and culture that they are trying to adjust to living in. Especially if you are leaving the culture you grew up in.

You see, not so very long ago I was in that place. It's now been over 7 years since I left the religious community I grew up in, only to get caught in another religious community and having to leave that one about 3 years ago. It's been a rough journey but I don't regret it for it has helped me to be more compassionate, sensitive and understanding of where others are coming from and what has brought them to the point where they are now.

My goal for this book is to share my own journey in the "fashion world" and share the things that have brought me to where I am now and hopefully it will be of help to you as well as give you room to record and process your journey as well.

I grew up as an Old Order Mennonite which means we drove horse and buggies for transportation and the women had to wear dresses with a cape (an extra piece of fabric on the front and back that reached from the neck to the waist) for "modesty" reasons.

Pants were considered men's attire because of Deuteronomy 22:5 which says: "The woman shall not wear that which pertaineth unto a man, neither shall a man put on a woman's garment: for all that do so are an abomination to God."

My mom would often take the neighbors' leftover yard sale stuff and store it in the basement and attic (I think her reasoning was something along the lines of trying to sell it the next year to make some extra money.) which then brought a lot of forbidden items into the house such as clothes that we were not allowed to wear. There were TVs and other items that the church didn't allow. Thus when my parents were away and we were left at home we would play dress up with the forbidden clothes.

One such time on a Sunday morning, my parents had gone to church and my one sister and I were left at home and we played dress-up, despite the fact that we were supposed to do our homework. I dressed up in jeans and a shirt and sat down to try to focus on my homework. The next thing I knew my stomach started hurting, intensely. After a while of the pain not lessening, I finally went and put my dress on again. That experience was marked in my memory as a young teen and I was convinced that God was punishing me by causing that pain for the longest time. Looking back now, I understand that my view of God was so twisted, fed by the fears of my mom as well as the teachings in the culture of my youth. It was not until I began to understand the truth about who God is and having a relationship with Him that I began to see that it wasn't God that was punishing me but rather my body was just trying to communicate something to me.

Jewelry also was a no-no. I remember at one point we had some green and purple mardi gras beads that were in the toybox and the younger siblings would use them as necklaces when playing with dolls.

The neighbor lady and her husband would often stop by with things for us. He was a cook in the school cafeteria of a nearby city and she was a kindergarten teacher. They were both kind-hearted Christians and as children we were always glad to see them because they treated us with kindness and love which was missing in our home. I still remember how one day she showed up with something on her way to school and she had huge yellow earrings on. As a young teen, I think I was shocked and maybe a bit horrified. Who in the world would think such huge bright earrings were even pretty?! I think it was just her way of style and now that I think about it totally matched her personality. She was very "alive and contagious".

As a young teen, I also learned to sew my own dresses. Now and then I had a dress I really liked as well as some I didn't like very well. I didn't have too much of a choice though because sometimes the fabric I liked was stuff that mom didn't think was appropriate. The guide she went by was that the print shouldn't be too much bigger than a quarter.

As an older teen in my culture, we started going with the youth around 17 ½ years old. Then I had girls I hung out with on the weekend and often for the summer our group would get "buddy" dresses, meaning that we would pick some fabric and then everyone would have a dress like it. We would then wear the dresses together at special events like supper crowds. (Supper crowds were held at a church family's place after instruction class which happened on Sunday afternoons 6-8 times through July and August for those who wanted to join the church.)

Also black was a predominant color. I hated it. It was so depressing and suffocating. According to church rules our hats, bonnets, jackets, sweaters, socks and shoes were supposed to be black. The ones who "rode the fence" would wear gray at times. Our everyday clothes at home could be other colors but still had to be dark.

Around maybe 8 years old some of my siblings and I went to my aunt and uncle's place for the weekend, not knowing till later that we were going to get a new sibling. That Sunday we went with them to church and since it was a more liberal church I was allowed to wear my cousin's white socks and a new dress my aunt had made for each of us. Those white socks left quite the impression on my young heart. I felt so pretty to be able to wear something other than black.

When I joined the church at 18 I was then eligible and expected to take part in communion which happened twice a year which meant that a black dress was added to my wardrobe. (Before a girl joined church they were expected to have a navy dress in their wardrobe for communion, even though they didn't take part. It also helped differentiate members and non-members for the bishop who passed out the elements of bread and wine.) This black dress was made in the same fashion as my other one with one difference. It needed to have an "apron" added to it which was basically the same size as the front half of the skirt, hemmed by hand, and fastened at the waist. (When a young lady got married she was expected to add an apron to all her "going away" and Sunday dresses. Single ladies were expected to add aprons to their dresses when they turned 30 or around that age. Boy, was I not looking forward to turning 30 because not only was I expected to put an apron on my dresses but I would also be expected to exchange my white covering strings for black ones! To me that meant I was an old lady!

This is basically the foundation of my experience in the fashion world as I knew it as a child and teen and the memories I have of my time in that culture. More things were not allowed than were allowed and I didn't know how to make the Bible and what I was taught line up. I accepted because that was what I was taught and I was supposed to be submissive. But it didn't stop me from having questions. I once asked my mom why we dress the way we do and why our head coverings are the way they are. The only answer I got was "We've always done it this way."

Years later, after I had left home and moved to a different community (but same culture) I had access to the library and did what research I could with the books I found and I was fascinated by what I discovered. The head covering styles were basically the same as what ladies wore in the 1500–1600's. The cape was not added to the dress till the early 1900's when ladies began to dress differently and it was an attempt to differentiate the Mennonites from the rest of the world, as before all the ladies basically dressed the same and it was the rich people that would embellish their clothes whereas the Mennonites and Amish would dress as plain as possible by wearing dark colors and no unnecessary embellishments that didn't add to the functionality of the article of clothing. So then, dictating what people could wear or not wear added to the control factor and now has the similitude of a cult because of the control and lack of information which allows abuse of every kind to grow into an epidemic unchecked behind the scenes.

What has your experience been like regarding clothing styles in your childhood and teenage years? Did you grow up in a religious culture that dictated what you wore? Who made your clothing choices for you? Or did you get to have free reign with a bit of your mom's advice and suggestions? How about taking some time and just jotting down your memories? I would like to walk with you on your fashion journey and the best way to start is in the beginning because we are influenced greatly by the things that happened in our early years. It is part of what makes us who we are. If you had a painful childhood, I would suggest finding a person you trust that can help you process and to discuss things with that is brought to the surface by the activities or stories that I share. I would highly recommend a trauma-informed professional because in my experience those who aren't trauma-informed can unintentionally add to the harm and abuse that we had to endure as children.

____

____

____

____

____

____

____

In this culture there were also rules about the hair and head covering. We were not allowed to cut our hair in any way, a rule which was based on 1 Corinthians 11:4-7 which says "Every man praying or prophesying, having his head covered, dishonoureth his head. But every woman that prayeth or prophesieth with her head uncovered dishonoureth her head: for that is even all one as if she were shaven. For if the woman be not covered, let her also be shorn: but if it be a shame for a woman to be shorn or shaven, let her be covered. For a man indeed ought not to cover his head, forasmuch as he is the image and glory of God: but the woman is the glory of the man." Girls under teenage years had their hair contained in two braids.

Occasionally mom would braid our hair in a french braid and sometimes for school we were allowed to wear ponytail bands that had beads on them. Fancy styles or trying new styles were discouraged.

When we washed our hair every other Saturday we were allowed to let it hang open to dry. We had some colored headbands that we were allowed to wear to keep our hair out of our face.

As a young child I enjoyed reading stories about the Indians and sometimes I would need to go outside to do something while my hair was drying and I would let the wind blow through my hair and dream of what it would be like to gallop across wild open spaces on a palomino or paint horse and feel my hair streaming in the wind.

When girls turned 13 they would start wearing their hair up in a bun. We had to wear a hairnet even though I know that there were others who didn't. I didn't like it because it bothered my head even though I had to get used to it because there was no other alternative. One of my younger sisters had such thick hair that mom took a big knife through her hair to thin it so it could be made manageable and fit under her covering. To me as a child with unanswered questions it was confusing because the church said to not cut hair and yet my mom did this? And to have all the "English" clothing that we weren't allowed to wear to begin with and yet you want to sell it and make money off of it? It didn't make sense to me then and neither does it now.

When I had braids mom would put a snap barrette in the front and another barrette behind my ear to keep all the stray ends in place. When I started wearing my hair up I started using bobby pins that were less visible under my covering. Everyone did a little differently, but in general your barrettes were supposed to be hidden under your head covering.

Our head coverings were made of a stiff mesh type fabric which had no other use that I know of except I was told it was used by surgeons to fix hernias. Now I don't know if that is true or not, but if it is there's a good chance that I have some in my body because I had to have hernia surgery as a 14 week old preemie.

The back part that covered our hair bun looked similar to a coffee filter. It was attached to a wide band that was supposed to come far enough forward to cover at least half our ears. Then we had ¼" white ribbon for the strings that we tied quite loosely under our chin, often dangling down between our chest and our throat. The married ladies (after they were married around 5 years) were expected to change the color to black as well as single ladies after they turned 30. The grandmas in the church who were used to an older style would use something similar to organdy fabric in white and made in a more boxy shape than the coffee filter type of the younger generation. The ribbon they used was between ¼" to ½" wide and tied snug under their chin as they often didn't use straight pins to hold their head coverings on like the younger generation does. Their coverings usually covered their ears completely.

Whenever we went away we would wear bonnets over our head coverings. If it wasn't Sunday our bonnets were usually a mesh or straw bonnet covered with a dark fabric with a small print. On Sunday or for other "Sunday best" functions like weddings and funerals we wore black bonnets that were made from some kind of black plastic and covered with black knit fabric. In the winter we would sometimes wear a black bandana underneath to try to protect our ears from the cold wind, especially if we were biking, which reminds me of so many times biking 5 miles to and from church in blustery freezing winter weather and having a numb face, feet and hands.

Our shoes were supposed to be all black. Our everyday shoes were other dark colors but anything we wore to go to functions in the church and community were supposed to be black. We could wear sneakers and Sketchers were popular. Our Sunday shoes had to be dress shoes without embellishments. As a young teen I remember wearing shoes that reminded me of a grandma's shoes. As an older teen, a girl wanted to dress like her friends and often that meant shoes with heels. Heels were not supposed to be more than an inch or two high and since most didn't have laces, dad would use a paper punch or other tool to punch 4 holes in the front so that a shoelace could be put in to have the appearance of laces so that it would be "in line" with the church rules.. And of course the church sanctuaries had no carpet so that meant you had to almost walk on your tiptoes in order to not make too much noise when you wore heels. The heels themselves were not supposed to be higher than one or two inches.

Our jackets and sweaters also had to be black. I remember
my mom taking a seam ripper and using it to take off
writing and decals on jackets as well as embellishments so
that the jacket would fit in the prescribed guidelines. So
much work just to fit in the box!

Part of our Sunday attire was also having to wear black
nylons. Sometimes the nylons got holes in them and instead
of throwing them away mom had a bottle of clear nail polish
on her dresser that we would use to put around the hole and
when it dried it would keep the hole from getting bigger.
One of the things I remember hearing was, "Ich hab en ku
chus za." translated would mean "I shot a cow", meaning that
my pair of nylons had a hole in it.. One of my younger
sisters would say that occasionally and there was often some
comeback though I don't remember what except maybe my
mom saying that "Now you better go skin her." I can't
remember if my group of youth girlfriends used that term
or not.

What is your experience with hair, outer wraps and shoes? Did you get to trim or cut your hair? Did your jackets and shoes have to be a certain color? Did you get to decide those things or did someone else make the decisions for you? Can you take some time to share your memories and the things that impacted you in these areas? Was Scripture twisted to make you stay under someone else's control?

____

____

____

____

____

____

____

____

____

____

____

____

____

____

It seems that God had to get me away from people and to live alone so that I would be brave enough to face the questions of my childhood. This was also around the time I gained access to the library. My employer at the time and his wife had gained my trust and taught me how to study the Bible. I wrote a letter or two to the ministry in the church to ask them questions. I finally came to the place where I got so tired of what people said was the right way and I asked God to show me how He wants me to live. He opened my eyes to how so many of the things I had been taught in my church and culture were non-existent in the Bible. The more I studied the more I began to see that I would be a hypocrite to continue going to a church I can no longer support and no longer agree with. That led to having to choose between following what God had shown me in the Bible or doing what my parents wanted me to do which was staying Mennonite. It was a really hard choice and will forever have repercussions because I chose to follow God instead of pleasing my parents. It also led to losing all the friends I thought I had. Not only did I have to leave the church and culture but I had to do it alone (with God) because I had no friends outside of the culture except those in the workplace.

My employer and his wife who had gained my trust took me under their wings so to speak and became spiritual parents in a way. They believed in the woman wearing a head covering and no pants the same as I did. I changed out my stiff head covering for a soft veil. I changed out my cape dress with a skirt and blouse or a jumper. Because their beliefs aligned with Pentecostal Holiness I started attending churches that aligned with those beliefs, eventually ending up in a church 3 hours away to which I drove every weekend unless I was sick or the weather too bad.

Under that influence I wore long sleeved shirts and long skirts to my ankles (which is my preference to begin with) and sometimes dresses but no cape dresses. They also equated jewelry with pride as I had been taught, therefore I didn't wear any. I was now free to wear whatever color clothes I wanted as well as shoes and jackets. It was so liberating!

What I didn't realize was that even though the services and culture were seemingly opposite, there were still guidelines. It wasn't until the pandemic hit in 2020 that I began to see that I am only going for the emotional high derived from the services and as an abuse survivor it was hard enough to figure out how to deal with my emotions let alone go to a church service that created emotional highs. Even though I continued to go almost till the end of the year there were finally a number of reasons that I knew I could not continue attending.

In this time period of realizing these things I came across a website called Berean Holiness. It was started by a brother and sister who had grown up in the same kind of church culture that I was in and had begun to see the twisted teachings of that culture and were writing articles about these things. There were two articles that I couldn't read for the longest time; namely, "Can Godly Women Wear Pants?" and "Jewelry On Trial". I think one of the reasons I found it hard to get the courage to read them was because I was afraid it would challenge everything I had been taught and I was not wrong. I mean, who likes having their worldview challenged or their entire belief system rooted up?

One Sunday morning my pastor's wife was talking to me about an individual that came to church and how this person just wasn't enlightened enough because she wore pants. According to that culture's belief, when a person gets right with God they would also apparently be convicted against wearing pants.

Another time she was talking of how one of the guys from church had gone to another country to do mission work and mentioning an Indian couple that was coming to church, she said that it is just so sad they just haven't had it revealed to them that jewelry is wrong and sinful to wear. She mentioned that in that other country (India) there are also holiness people similar to this church but they just don't know how bad it is to wear jewelry. They just haven't been enlightened. The way she said it turned my stomach because she was implying that jewelry was a pride and sin item that real Christians don't wear as well, implying that this church is the only right church and anyone outside of the culture was considered as less than and well, dumb, because apparently in this church we've had more knowledge revealed to us and we are holier because we don't cut our hair or wear pants. It reeked like pride to me and put a bitter taste in my mouth. I wasn't bold enough to disagree so I just kept my mouth shut because I didn't want to be seen as a backslider which most definitely would have happened.

It was around this time that I finally read those articles. The arguments were rooted in Scripture and study of the land and culture when the Bible was written and refuted the arguments for the current traditions. I began to see how Scripture had once again been so twisted and vague verses turned into legalistic traditions in order to control and set the group apart from the outside "English" world.

I could no longer support the things I was being taught, nor did I have enough finances to keep driving that far for church, so I found a Calvary Chapel church nearby to go to. I also realized I knew nothing about styles or how to dress and so I did some research to see if I can figure out my personal style which we will get into in the next chapter.

How has your fashion journey been? Did it go by steps like it has for me? Perhaps take some time to write down the memories and thoughts that have come to your mind as you read about my journey. Do you see similarities? Or perhaps you've always had the freedom to wear pants and jewelry?

____

____

____

____

____

____

____

____

____

____

____

____

____

____

What Is Your Skin Tone

When I was around 18 or so, a Mennonite friend and I were walking along the road. She picked a wildflower and held it up. "This reminds me of you," she said, "small and dainty."

At the time I knew nothing about having a personal style or even that there was something like that. What I do know is that down through the years those words came to mind whenever I was choosing something; whether it was picking dress fabric for my next new dress or designing my dream home. (I have searched and searched but cannot figure out the name of the plant. It is similar to bedstraw but much more fragile in appearance.)

After I left the Mennonites I wore skirts and blouses and I enjoyed the freedom of picking clothes to wear. I would buy things and then after wearing them a time or two I would often realize that I didn't like it whether it was the color or the make of it or even just the type of fabric.. I often felt like I wasted money and made me frustrated and discouraged at times. On the good side it helped me figure out what I liked and didn't like to a certain degree, enough to help me start figuring out what I liked and didn't like.

One day I got the idea from somewhere to see what I can find online to help me figure out what color and styles of clothing would best be for me. One of the first things I found was that your skin has an underlying color tone and that determines what colors look best on you.

There is much information online so I'll try to describe as simply as possible: your skin has either a cool, warm, or neutral tone and there are several ways to determine what yours is.

1.   Vein test:

Check out the veins on the underside of your wrists. If they are blue or purple in color, you probably have a cool undertone. If they are greenish, then you have a warm undertone. If you find it difficult to decide which it is then you may have a neutral tone.

2.   Jewelry or Gold & Silver Foil test:

How does your skin look when you hold gold jewelry to it? Does it look flattering or sick? If it seems to compliment your skin well then you probably have a warm skin tone. What about silver? If it looks well on you then you probably have a cool skin tone. If both look good on you then you probably have a neutral skin tone.

3.   White Paper test:

Hold up a piece of white paper under your jaw while looking in the mirror. If your skin looks yellowish then you probably have a warm tone. If your skin looks pinkish then you probably have a cool skin tone.

4.   Sun Test:

How well do you tan in the sunshine without burning? If you tan easily without burning, you may have a warm or neutral tone. Otherwise you probably have a cool skin tone.

5.   Color test:

Hold your clothes up to your face and see which ones make your skin look good. If colors like blue look well with your skin color then you may have a cool skin tone. If colors of yellow look well against your skin then you have a warm skin tone. If any color looks good with your skin tone then you probably have a neutral skin tone.

You may be wondering why you would want to know your skin tone... if you haven't figured it out yet the wrong color can make you look pale or sick. There are many types of combinations that go well together. It just takes a bit of time to figure out your personal style.

I'm a bit of a perfectionist so it was hard to figure out exactly what my skin tone was. Blue is my favorite color and so I began to hold different colored clothes up to my face to see which ones look better. Now and then I've also had people compliment me and tell me that I look good in a certain color and that helps me become even more aware of what colors compliment my skin tone.

*Have you tried any of the tests to find your skin tone yet?
Have some fun and try them, one or all. Then write down
your thoughts on each of your experiments. Do you have a
favorite color, or one that you hate? Can you figure out why
you love or hate those colors? How do they make you feel if
you wear one or the other?*______________________________

____

____

____

____

____

____

____

____

____

____

____

____

____

____

Figuring Out Your Body Shape

One of the things that I did, I don't remember if it was before or after I did some research on what colors go together, was to see if I can figure out what kind of clothes fit well to my body shape. There are several different body shapes: pear/triangle, hourglass/curvy, apple/inverted triangle, and athletic/rectangle or straight shape. For some people, loose and gathered clothing flatters their body shape; and for others, contoured and close fitting clothing looks good.

I am short of stature with a medium build and I like to often wear baggy clothing because of growing up in a purity culture where women were objectified and made to be responsible for the men's potential to lust. It made me so self conscious and fed some of my wildest fears. And feeling that I was to be blamed for rape and assault if it happened because somehow it would have been my fault because of the clothes I wore or the way I acted that may have caused a man to lust and lose control of himself. But so I was taught and so it was implied in many different ways. I know now "in my head" that a man's actions are not my responsibility but I am still dealing with the emotional and mental beliefs and repercussions of living in such a culture.

I took some time to research and read different fashion stories about celebrities and their ways of choosing clothing to help me figure out what the best options are for someone like me. It opened a whole new world for me and helped me narrow down my clothing choices to some that will go well with my body shape rather than baggy clothing or styles that made me look worse than reality. I like to dress well and feel dressed up even though basically all my clothing comes from thrift shops. Looking at how other people do it helped me get an idea of how to go about it and also helped me isolate the better options, helping me not feel quite as overwhelmed.

Even though I'd love to show pictures, most are probably copyrighted so instead I will give you links where you can explore for yourself at your own pace:

https://gabriellearruda.com/how-to-dress-better-female-body-shape/

https://www.stitchfix.com/women/blog/fashion-tips/find-fit-for-your-body-type/

https://www.stylecraze.com/articles/right-clotnes-for-body-type/

https://allthedresses.com.au/blog/a-guide-to-dressing-for-your-body-type

https://www.matchclothing.co.uk/whats-my-body-shape.html

https://www.glamcorner.com.au/blog/how-to-dress-for-your-body-shape

https://www.whowhatwear.com/how-to-dress-for-body-type-pear-apple-hourglass

Once you figure out what your body type is then take some time to research that specific body type and how people have dressed that type of body in a way that looks good. For example, if your body is what is considered an apple shape, then an article like this would be a good place to start:
https://theconceptwardrobe.com/build-a-wardrobe/apple-body-shape
Or a pear body shape:
https://theconceptwardrobe.com/build-a-wardrobe/apple-body-shapetheconceptwardrobe.com/build-a-wardrobe/pear-body-shape
There are so many directions one could go. It just takes a little bit to figure out just how and what direction is best for you.

If you would rather have a physical book to read rather than going online here are some that you may find

interesting and may be able to find them at your library:
-The Body Shape Bible by Trinny & Susannah
-Your Body Shape by Waistplacement (a 19 book series)
-Color Your Style by David Zyla

Do you know what your body type is? What are your favorite kinds of clothes to wear? Do they fit your body type? What are some changes you would like to make in your wardrobe? Did you learn something new in this chapter? Or perhaps you have your own ideas...why not take some time to jot down the things that have caught your attention or even questions you may have or things you are curious about?

Finding Your Color Palette

After I figured out what my skin tone might be and realized that I like soft but alive-looking colors, I went on Pinterest to see what I could find to help me know what colors to go for. Since I like spring colors as well, I discovered that there is also something called the four seasons palette which I will share in a little bit. There are just so many varieties out there that it's hard to not get overwhelmed: but then, that's why I'm writing about my fashion journey in hopes that it will help you get started and not feel so overwhelmed at the sheer amount of information out there...

If you do a simple internet search for color charts to give you an idea which colors might go together and which ones might clash it will help you a lot. If you know which colors compliment your skin type you might find some new colors to use and learn how to blend different ones together to create a stunning style for yourself, because after all, clothing really does affect your thoughts about yourself in case you haven't picked up on that...

There are also some four seasonal palettes that can help you get started. There are also numerous versions of each one as well, so if you know which season or group matches you best then you can springboard from there and explore that group's varieties. It's really fun but can get overwhelming too. Sometimes I had to just stop, put away my phone and go look at the clothes in my closet (or doing something unrelated instead in totally okay too) and figure out what I could pair with what I have as well as what had to be disposed of. Here are links to help you get an idea:

1.   Winter palette colors:

https://theconceptwardrobe.com/colour-analysis-comprehensive-guides/true-winter-a-comprehensive-guide

https://colorhunt.co/palettes/winter

https://thelaurieloo.com/blog/seasonal-color-analysis

https://www.kettlewellcolours.co.uk/blog/jo/winter-explaining-the-different-types

https://offeo.com/learn/winter-color-palette

https://goplaycosmetics.com/blogs/colorcreateloveplay/the-12-color-seasons-winter-and-its-subsets

2.   Spring palette colors:

https://colorhunt.co/palettes/spring

https://theconceptwardrobe.com/colour-analysis-comprehensive-guides/true-spring-a-comprehensive-guide

https://www.kettlewellcolours.co.uk/blog/jo/spring-explaining-the-different-types

https://goplaycosmetics.com/blogs/colorcreateloveplay/the-12-color-seasons-spring-and-its-subsets

https://looka.com/blog/spring-color-palettes/

https://www.style-yourself-confident.com/seasonal-color-analysis-spring.html

3. *Summer palette colors:*

https://theconceptwardrobe.com/colour-analysis-comprehensive-guides/true-summer-a-comprehensive-guide

https://colorhunt.co/palettes/summer

https://www.kettlewellcolours.co.uk/blog/jo/summer-explaining-the-different-types

https://www.style-yourself-confident.com/seasonal-color-analysis-summer.html

https://goplaycosmetics.com/blogs/colorcreateloveplay/the-12-color-seasons-summer-and-its-subsets

http://cardiganempire.com/2017/02/best-worst-colors-for-summer-seasonal-color-analysis.html

4.   Autumn palette color:
https://yourcolorguru.com/are-you-an-autumn/

https://theconceptwardrobe.com/colour-analysis-comprehensive-guides/true-autumn-a-comprehensive-guide

https://www.kettlewellcolours.co.uk/blog/jo/autumn-explaining-the-different-types

https://goplaycosmetics.com/blogs/colorcreateloveplay/the-12-color-seasons-autumn-and-its-subsets

https://thelaurieloo.com/blog/autumn-color-palette

https://maniology.com/blogs/maniology-blog/autumn-color-palette

Here are some books if you're interested in going that route instead:

-Seasonal Color Analysis: Find the Best Colors For Your Skin Tone by Namrata Italiya

-Color Me A Season: A Complete Guide to Finding Your Best Colors and How to Use Them by Bernice Kentner

-Color Revival: Understanding the 12 Season Color Analysis System by Lori Alexander

What are you thinking by now? Are you getting overwhelmed? If you are, it's ok for you to put this book down and take some to process and digest all I've shared with you so far. Is there anything in particular that stood out to you? What colors do you tend to reach for? Those might be a hint for a place to start and then see if you can find other colors that go well with them. How about taking some time to write out your thoughts to help you process these big bites of color?________________________________

____

____

____

____

____

____

____

____

____

____

____

Decision Time

I often stand by my closet in the morning and sometimes it takes me the longest time to figure out what to wear, especially when I'm trying to dress up for a special event. When you haven't had a voice or been free to choose for most of your life, it can be very hard to make decisions in the smallest details of life, and that would entail clothing. I don't know about you but it's been a rough struggle some days going through my whole closet, fitting on different things and trying to figure out what I feel like wearing and often I'd end up wearing something I didn't really like because I ran out of time.

One thing I do occasionally is to hang certain outfits together. That way, when you are short on time you have something to fall back on. Other days when I just want to be comfortable I just wear whatever I feel like wearing. Some days your body needs that space to relax and not be careful of how your clothes look or if they get dirty. It may be fun to dress up but it is also good to take the space we need to be ourselves without pressure.

I believe that the clothes we wear should make us feel good. I have been surprised at how pretty clothes that I like make me feel more confident as well as happier. Wearing clothes that make you feel depressed, sad, or any other negative way may have an impact on whether you have a good day or not. Granted, we do at times choose to wear clothes that match our mood. There's nothing wrong

 with that. It may in fact help us become more aware of what we are feeling and then we need to make space to deal with the root of it so that it doesn't control the outcome of our day. It is our responsibility to find ways to heal those parts of us that are hurting and clamoring for our attention. That may look overwhelming to you at this point and if you don't know who to reach out to, you may reach out to me and I will see if I can help you find the right resources and connections to help you. It takes a lot of courage and bravery to reach out for help, but I will have contact information in the back so that you will have a way of contacting me.

Hopefully by now you have some ideas forming in your mind of what might be your personal style and colors. It took me quite a few years to get to the place where I am today. It was a gradual journey. I now try to not think so much about the money I wasted on clothes but rather look at it as a learning experience. In every learning experience you make mistakes as you learn what is the best procedure or style or whatever the experience may be about.

As an abuse survivor, it can be extremely hard to accept yourself and your body. I have found that wearing clothes that make me feel good, it also helps me to accept myself a little more. If you find yourself hating yourself, there's usually a reason. Sometimes it takes a while to uncover those reasons. I have some of my own and you are not alone if you find yourself in this place. There are other survivors who find themselves in this place as well but I do find that the more I heal the less I hate who I am. It also helps to cut negative people out of your life if possible, because that will drain your energy as well. Another important thing is having the right kind of support. If you don't know how to get started in these things, but want to take steps to move forward and heal, you may also contact me for these things and I would be happy to help you get connected with people who will encourage and support you.

Here's a book that may help:
-Classic Style by Kate Schelter

What are your thoughts by now? Do you find it hard to choose your clothes like I do? Have you found your clothing choices to affect your day? Are there bad things that happened to you that make it hard to like yourself and your body? Have you taken any steps to heal? If not, what is holding you back? Is there some way you wish that someone would help you? Do you have someone you could ask to help you find the right person to meet your needs?

____

____

____

____

____

____

____

____

____

____

____

____

Hair Styles

I mentioned before how I had my hair in braids and also up in a bun when I was part of the Mennonite church. When I went to the holiness Pentecostal church I wore a veil but I would let my hair in a ponytail. One lady thought it would look so pretty if I would braid my long hair but little did she know that I used to have to wear my hair in braids and I prefer to not generally because it reminds me of the past.

I have discovered that if I keep my hair moisturized enough, it actually gets wavy. I did some research and found different things to help my hair. Shea Moisture is one of my favorite brands.

Generally, I leave my hair hanging. Sometimes I use a tiny hair clip on the side so my hair stays out of my face when I'm trying to work. Now and then I'll braid my hair down the back just to get it back while letting some waves go free so it doesn't remind me of the past too much like it does when I have my hair pulled straight back. Other times I will use a barrette at the base of my neck to keep the majority of hair in the back so that it doesn't get in the way. Pinterest has also given me a lot of ideas but most of them I can't do by myself. Most of the ideas are also for the back of your head with your hair pulled back which again reminds me of the past.

I used to put my hair in a big hair clip on the back but I'm so sensitive that I can't leave my hair up for a whole day. The same with using a barrette. Or a ponytail band. Instead I will often just use a tiny clip on the one side to keep some of the hair out of my face.

There's many other things that you can do to help your hair be at its best. I trim my hair when the ends start splitting and becoming scraggly. It also feels better on my scalp when my hair isn't as long.

My suggestion would be to choose one thing to make your hair better, whether it's too dry or frizzy or whatever you struggle with and then do some research on what may be the causes and choose one natural way to "empower" your hair to be its best. It's self care, taking care of your body, and helping you feel better about yourself.

My recommendation:

-SheaMoisture....they are fair trade as well as try to avoid harsh chemicals

-the item I use the most is called Coconut & Hibiscus Curl & Style Milk

There is also something called the Curly Girl Method. I have found several articles that have helped me figure out what kind of hair products are the best and healthiest for my hair. Also everyone's hair is different so what works for me might not be the best for you; but if you want a place to start you can try what I like and branch out from there, hopefully without being overwhelmed because things like this can be overwhelming especially in the beginning when you are just starting out trying to take better care of yourself.

The first article is called Curly Girl Method Silicones to Avoid and here is the link to type into your browser:

https://likelovedo.com/curly-girl-method-silicones-to-avoid/

The next one I found is called Drying Alcohols to Avoid in CG Method and here is the link:

https://likelovedo.com/drying-alcohols-to-avoid-in-cg-method/

One of my counselors told me she uses sea salt spray to help her hair have beach waves so I found an article about the best ones to use but now that I have looked at the ingredients there are some ingredients that don't fit in the accepted list of the above mentioned 2 articles. The one I got was called Not Your Mother's Beach Babe Texturizing Sea Salt Spray. The first attempt was a flop. I sprayed it on and scrunched my hair with my hands while running out the door to an appointment. What would probably have worked better would be to spray it on and then plop my hair in a towel or find some other way to scrunch it in curls till it dries. Even though I tried it that way the second time I felt like it dried my hair out and made it somewhat stiff. It seems similar to hairspray which I don't use because I hate

the smell and it affects my body negatively, probably from the chemicals in it. I will probably get rid of it because I don't like the way it makes my hair feel. Here is the link to the list if you want to try one:
https://www.cosmopolitan.com/style-beauty/beauty/g27442711/salt-spray-hair/

There are many different items and collections out there to try. What will take the most time is doing your research based on what you want to support such as fair trade or no testing on animals. More and more I'm getting to the place where I want to avoid putting any chemicals in or on my body. I'm only at the beginning of my journey I'd say and the more research and studies come out and things get uncovered, I'm sure my choices will change as well. This is to help you get started right where you are and make responsible and informed choices to help you be the best version of yourself you can be.

Here are some books that you may find interesting:
-The 25 Rules for Natural Hair Care by Olivia Atembina
-Curly Girl The Handbook by Lorraine Massey & Michele Bender
-To Hell Hair and Back by Rhonda Eason
-90 Days to Beautiful Hair by Crystal Aguh, MD
-Secret of Healthy Hair by La Fonceur
-Hair Care Secrets with Natural Recipes by Vicks Anderson

-365 Days of Moisture for Dry & Parched Hair by Abi Faniren
-Natural Hair Coloring by Christine Shabin
-Hair Care Journal by Rosanna Orbk
-Curls, Curls, Curls by Samantha Harris
-If You Love It, It Will Grow by DR. Phoenyx Austin
-Get Your Length by Sais Sharpe
-Hair Rules by A. Dickey

Where are you at with your hair? What are the things you wish were different about your hair? What would your ideal hair look and feel like? Do you care about what you use on your hair or would you rather just use the cheapest stuff? Perhaps that's all you can afford and there's no shame in that. What has brought you to those conclusions? Is it something you have been taught or implied by those close to you? If you could do as you want with your hair, what would that look like?

Now comes the fun part! I have not yet tried makeup but would like to eventually. The main reason I haven't yet is because of hormonal acne which I was afraid would become even worse if I did. So what I would like to do is give resources and suggestions that I think would be helpful for myself when I would want to (and am brave enough to) get started.

First, here are a few articles that look helpful:
-18 Makeup Tips For Beginners
https://makeup.allwomenstalk.com/makeup-tips-for-beginners/

-Basic Makeup Tips And Tricks: 30 Absolute Need-To-Knows For Beginners
https://thebeautydeeplife.com/basic-makeup-tips-and-tricks/
There's a lot more out there and I assume everyone has their own style and ways of choosing and using makeup that can only be solidified by practice. And practice makes perfect or so it is said to do...

The other day I was putting out some nail polish at work. On the bottle it said plant based and so I wondered if it is different from the cheap nail polish. It smelled the same, with the same strong scent of chemicals that I don't like. Pondering this I began to wonder if there are any organic or chemical-free versions or brands out there, so I did some searching and I found some items that I would like to try. Now these items are much more expensive than the cheap drug store or thrift store versions; therefore if you want the better, healthier options like me then you may have to save up money to buy some which is what I intend to do simply because I know I feel better all around when I use things that are good for my body.

Next I offer to you the suggestions that I would be willing to try. Some are outside the country which may affect the price and shipping even more. Here are some lists:
-The 20 Best Natural Makeup Brands, According To Beauty Editors
https://www.womenshealthmag.com/beauty/g25361619/best-natural-makeup-brands/
-15 Organic Makeup Brands For Clean Cosmetics In 2023
https://www.thegoodtrade.com/features/18-natural-organic-makeup-brands-your-face-will-love-you-for
-12 Best Natural & Organic Makeup Brands
https://www.organicbeautylover.com/makeup/best-natural-organic-makeup-brands/

I don't know about you but this is more than enough information for me to get started. I'd probably choose the simplest easiest thing to start with like maybe some blush or eyeliner. But then again, I tend to go for the complicated things which more often tend to flop instead of really work out, leaving me frustrated and discouraged at times...it's just how I do more times than not because it seems like challenges give me a thrill. In a way, it's addictive but I'm thinking it could be from growing up in a dysfunctional home and no longer having that stress in my life, it almost seems like I have to create challenges in order to give my brain a work out since it's no longer being stretched by trying to survive all the time. This is my theory but it could be tied in with other things like perhaps autism which may or may not be a part of me. I do not have an official diagnosis but can identify with a lot of symptoms of other autistic people.

Sometimes I see people with excessive makeup and I wonder if they are hurting or are trying to cover up the hurt of life. I remember one time being at a cafe and the waiter had bright pink eyeliner. I admit I found it hard not to stare but underneath I wondered what caused her to use those colors; if that is just what she wanted to wear that day or if she was trying to cover up hurt and pain. What was the motivation? Sometimes it takes a little digging to figure it out for ourselves.

If you would like some books on the subject of makeup, here you go:

-Glow From Within by Joanna Vargas

-My Improbable Career in Magazines & Makeup by Jean Godfrey-June
-Radical Reinvention: Reimagine, Reset, Reinvent in a Disruptive World by Maureen Lippe
-Making Faces by Kevyn Aucoin
-Eat Beautiful by Wendy Rowe
-Face Forward by Kevyn Aucoin
-Teenage Beauty by Bobbi Brown

Have you tried makeup already? Has it been a good or bad experience? What are you looking for in makeup? What would you like to try? Do you have any beauty models you follow? Where would you like to go with this? Is something holding you back from going forward in this direction? Why not take some time to write out your thoughts and sort through the pros and cons of what this experience might be like for you...

Pretty Fingers

I like to use nail polish. It makes my fingers feel more slender but that might just be a mental thing. I have nine individual colors currently. Some I got from the thrift store, others came from the dollar store. My favorite one is the one my sister gave me which is a shimmering white nail lacquer.

The other day when I was trying to find some organic products I found some nail polish/lacquer I would like to try. A regular size bottle was priced at $18! Now I understand that it takes more work to try to make things organically or naturally because you can't just use the cheap chemicals that are put in the regular nail polish/lacquer. I appreciate the people who go to so much effort to try to make healthy products to replace the regular items that have all kinds of chemicals in them.

One time I bought some nail polish remover and what drew my attention and helped me make the choice were the words on the front of the label that said "Makes Nails Stronger". When I got home I was reading more on the label because I was curious how it can make nails stronger when it is stripping paint off your fingernails. On the back it says it can irritate the skin and to keep out of reach of children and pets. I must say I felt a little bit ripped off by the label portraying a false image and made me resolve to be even more careful of what I buy to put on or in my body. I am getting in the habit of reading the ingredients and back of labels before I even put it in my cart.

I have never been to a spa or salon of any type because somehow I could never justify spending money for such things when I had more important things I wanted to do with my money. I figured out how to do some of these things by myself which is empowering. Who doesn't like being independant? I guess there's all kinds of people but I also know that one thing that can play into it is that coming from an abusive home or relationship you learned to not trust people because you got hurt too many times. I know it is one of the factors that plays a role in my being independent. But there's nothing wrong with being independent. In fact, I think it's great because it helps you develop new skills and learn to solve problems on your own at times which can be great for survival if ever needed.

Here are some of the articles and brands I found that are supposed to be clean, natural and organic. I definitely want to try some of these. Right now I have the Londontown website bookmarked because they are US based and their items wouldn't need to be shipped internationally. I may change my mind before I get as far as buying one of their products, especially if I could find a store nearby that carries the same items but I haven't researched that far yet at this point.

-Best Natural Nail Polish 2022: 10 Organic Nail Polish Brands We Recommend

https://www.ecofriendlyhabits.com/best-natural-organic-nail-polish/

-10 Best Non-Toxic Nail Polishes for a Healthy Mani

https://www.goodhousekeeping.com/beauty/nails/g28834890/best-natural-non-toxic-nail-polishes/

(I really like what I see in this article. I didn't realize that nail polish can have so many toxic chemicals in it even though I suspected as much.)

-2023 Buying Guide: Best Non Toxic Nail Polish Brands

https://thenewknew.com/best-nontoxic-nail-polish-brands/

-This one has a bit of a different perspective by saying there is no such thing as chemical free or organic nail polish. It can be confusing with so many different ideas, experiences and information out there but this is just a bit of a different angle to aid you in your decisions.

-List of 10+ Eco-Friendly Nail Polish Brands; Non-Toxic & Vegan

https://ethicalelephant.com/eco-friendly-nail-polish/

Here are some books you may be interested in on the simple subject of nail polish:

-Nails: The Story of Modern Manicure by Suzanne E. Shapiro
-Nail Art Designing Book: Journal For Practicing Nail Art with 12 Different Nail Shapes by Jonny Publishing
-DIY Nail Art by Catherine Rodgers
-Spectacular Nail Art: A Step-by-Step Guide to 35 Gorgeous Designs by Larit Levy
-Homemade Nail Polish by Allison Rose Spiekermann

Do you like to use nail polish? Do you have any favorite colors? Is there something you would like to change in this area? Do you have a certain brand you like to use? Have you found a brand you would like to try? What is helping you make that decision?

Know the Difference, Choose Your Size

I have a friend who once told me how hard it was to figure out what clothing sizes to wear and so I'm thinking that may be a helpful thing to include. I have just always fitted every piece on to make sure it fits so that I don't waste my money for something that doesn't fit.

Men and women's clothing are different for the most part though that may be changing with all the gender fluidity that is happening in society today. One thing is the fit and cut. Men's clothing tends to be looser and more straight lines while women's clothing tends to be more curvy and have more things added like lace and ruffles. Patterns and colors are usually different too. Men's accessories tend to be more functional while women's accessories tend to be more stylish and various designs. Men's clothing is made to be more functional whereas women's clothing is more to create a statement and show a woman's style.

One thing to look for is where are the buttons located? Are they on the left or right? If you wear men's shirts the buttons are on the right side. If you wear women's shirts the buttons are on the left side.

For pants it can be difficult too. One way to tell the difference is the size. Women's pant sizes are a single even number beginning at zero. Men's pant sizes have two numbers: one is for the waist and the other is for the inseam. Another way to tell is how they fit. Men's pants will be more relaxed in the hips and waist whereas women's pants will be more fitted. A third way to tell at times is by the fabric. Men's pants are usually made from tougher fabrics while women's pants are made from softer, more delicate fabrics. A fourth way to help tell the difference is the style. Men's pants are usually more simple while women's pants can be more decorated and detailed. Men's pants are also more boxy and straight while women's pants are more fitted and flared.

Here are some blog posts you may find interesting:

https://zoneicon.com/men-and-women-clothing-understanding-thedifferences/

https://www.smithsonianmag.com/smart-news/heres-why-mens-and-womens-clothes-button-opposite-sides-1-180957361/

https://pantsshortsshoes.com/pants/mens-or-womens/

https://corporate.customthreadsandsports.com/blog/difference-mens-womens-shirts

Different brands have different sizes in pants so it's not possible to give a one-tecnique-fits-all suggestion or way of doing it. First you can measure your waist where you want the pants to sit on your body. Place the measuring tape around your waist at that level against your skin, but not too tight. Next, measure the inseam from the very top of the inside of your leg down to your ankle bone. When you have your numbers, find a conversion chart. You can find them online and are easy to use. Because sizing and brand vary from brand to brand, it will be best to go to the brand you want to buy and use their conversion chart.

I'm not sure I can offer too much more than that. I always try on the clothing I'd like to buy because I usually tend to regret it if I don't. I hope this gives you a place to start to find the right fit and style for you and your body that will present you as the beautiful person that you are no matter what you have been through.

<h1 style="text-align:center">Closing Comments</h1>

Thanks for joining me on this journey and letting me be a part of your journey. It may not have been easy but I hope you found something that was of help to you. I would love to hear from you and to know what was of help to you or even perhaps what you were looking for and didn't find. I only know what my journey was like so hearing other people's stories, needs, or questions would help me to know how I might be able to meet the needs, which I would love to do...

You can contact me through my website:

https://www.lighthopetruth.com/

www.ingramcontent.com/pod-product-compliance
Lightning Source LLC
Chambersburg PA
CBHW061323120726
48001CB00002B/667